Edna

poems by

Melissa Boston

Finishing Line Press
Georgetown, Kentucky

Edna

Copyright © 2022 by Melissa Boston
ISBN 978-1-64662-796-7 First Edition
All rights reserved under International and Pan-American Copyright Conventions. No part of this book may be reproduced in any manner whatsoever without written permission from the publisher, except in the case of brief quotations embodied in critical articles and reviews.

ACKNOWLEDGMENTS

Thank you to the following publications, where these poems first appeared, sometimes in different versions and with different titles:

Moon City Review: "Pastime: A narrative," "I have fantasies about the post office worker on 8th street," "For my brother," and "Soutine, your *Carcass*"
Raleigh Review: "—Continuum," and "[There and here]"
Midwestern Gothic: "[I will die in a Walmart parking lot]"
Four Ties Lit Review: "[When you arrived]"
I-70 Review: "within their constructed pastoral"
Blue Mesa Review: "Edna," and "Below the Organ Mountains"
The Fourth River Review: "[And we've slept for too long]"
Driftwood Press: "Small Cento: Edna finds a lover for tonight"
PMS: "Edna: Sleeping at Grand Isle"
These Fragile Lilacs: "Wind Poppy"
Bird's Thumb: "Rilke, your garden"

Publisher: Leah Huete de Maines
Editor: Christen Kincaid
Cover Art: Patrick Tucker
Author Photo: Patrick Tucker
Cover Design: Elizabeth Maines McCleavy

Order online: www.finishinglinepress.com
also available on amazon.com

Author inquiries and mail orders:
Finishing Line Press
PO Box 1626
Georgetown, Kentucky 40324
USA

Table of Contents

Edna, ... 1

[You think of an island] 2

[And we've slept for too long] 3

Edna: Sleeping at Grand Isle 4

[When you arrived] 5

Wind Poppy 6

Below the Organ Mountains 7

—Lordsburg, NM 8

Small Cento: Edna finds a lover for tonight 9

Soutine, your *Carcass* 10

Rilke, your garden 11

—That one winter when it snowed everywhere 12

Pastime: A narrative 14

Edna's Incantation: Or, how I imagine 15

—There and here 16

[The day begins in rain] 18

Trakl Speaks: 20

—I have fantasies about the post office worker on 8th St 21

—Assignation 22

But afterwards: 23

—Continuum 24

Trakl, your self-portrait 25

Before the autopsy 26

For my brother 27

[I will die in a Walmart parking lot] 28

within their constructed pastoral 30

Notes 31

Thank Yous 33

Edna,

I thought I'd find you here eating a pear,
staring at the desert ground waiting
to see if it would break apart into ants

carrying seeds to you. To see if the empty
creek with its shadow-current cut into sand
would fill with rain that was supposed to come
but didn't—the weather is off by a day

here. Tell me how before you left home
you made sure the porch lights were off
because he and you weren't returning there.
How you woke in other beds, in other places,

and how he became someone else who answers
to the same name darkness left behind. Tell me, Edna.

[You think of an island]

You think of an island, where heavenly light filters
through the palms as clear as the coconut milk
served by local girls, where the ghostly hull
of a 40s oil tanker is beached, discontent
under the trades coming through the channel,
like a descending osprey quickly tearing into flesh.
Some days, you thought, nothing is as aptly named.

You think of this island as I think of you,
sea-circled, remote, and conquered by near-
hidden ill-tempered elements, an island too,
with languorous thoughts approaching
the blue waters to find its dark coral
and breaking at the base. My wanted Kaiolohia,

some days you thought nothing except the motion
of those waves and a few gulls with lurid cries.

[And we've slept for too long]

And we've slept for too long
in our rented bed, next to long windows.
What is it we've overlooked? Your island
looms between the horizon and the sea line—
but you will not miss your ferry.
It will arrive on time. You will leave early.

We must have slept for too long
because we were lost in ourselves,
remained too long in our lull.
We moved our rented bed closer
to our long rented windows, slept
with our backs to your growing island.
We moved the rented furniture around.

Clearly a lot's been going on
and we've refused to recognize it.
Our bills gathering in individual trays
at separate post offices. We will collect them
when we wake in other places. I will leave
on a delayed flight that will bring me
to tomorrow five hours earlier

than you will have to wake. It's not just
a matter of time zones. It's not just
a matter of long silences. We've simply
slept for too long, tormented by currency
of bought time: I overlooked you
closing the curtains. You overlooked me
closing the door to our rented room.

Edna: Sleeping at Grand Isle

What else could she be but body
parts laid out, naked, on white
sheets that swallow her?

The sea-mouth dampened by sweat,
I would part only those lips
to save her. With the single touch of my finger-

tip to that soft sea the salt would gather
into a solid mass. How many creatures,
ourselves included, would come to lick it down

when awakened? Her body breaks into water
only to dry into the winding sheeted-sea.

[When you arrived]

When you arrived at my apartment by Kaanapali
you came with your backpack and Buffalo Trace.
We poured drinks, sat on rented patio furniture,
and ate the pineapple and ohi'a 'ai I brought

from the bar down the beach link. That morning
you agreed to stay two more nights before leaving.
And I would often wake to find you lost in dreams,
shivering from some undeliverable message.

By the last morning I wanted to imagine you
staying one more night; sitting across from me
talking about the golden sands of Manele Bay;
and everything I imagine of your days there
is what I want you to be: easy and clear.

I think I must have wanted you to return
with me to the mainland, but down by the docks,
in August, the warm rain would not hide the truth
from me for long. Fate was the saltwater between us,
under still perfect skies, in which must have risen,
sometimes, the low ghosts of absent desert mountains.

Wind Poppy

Apricot gold,
hot copper
flame of bitter-
sweet melon
wedge of cantaloupe,
California sun-
set in grass-
lands, blooming
mid-April
from fire's orange-
red embers.
How easily
you're broken.

Below the Organ Mountains

Tonight she is tall enough to see
the green light surrounding him

fade into a silver oval to pluck from
the fastened sky. Overripe,
his calloused rind

should peel away from his flesh,
so all that is left is him, camphor

odor and octagon-sacs of sap,
broken to consume. A creosote
continues to flower in winter

when others fold into themselves
like batwings. The desert starts here,

with the lights of some distant city
too far away that they are mistaken
for fixed stars. He grows as she

approaches, eddying to a dissolve,
returning to green light.

—**Lordsburg, NM**

The sun blisters the sky
and diseases it with hues
of pink. I haven't seen

a blue dawn since I left
home. Pinning photographs

to the muntin bars I stare
farther past the edges
of desert continents.

The sun is inflating
into a hot air balloon,

its basket still
carrying the same person
I try not to recognize,

floating in the forming scar.
I've become sentimental,

but am too dehydrated
to cry. The eastern edge
of the field bursts into a frost

of cornsilk lighted windows,
coldly holding dust particles

leftover from the storm.
And as the balloon deflates
into the darkening desert,

I try not to look for you.
We've been wanting

to believe in our ability
that we could say it
without having to ask.

Small Cento: Edna finds a lover for tonight

This is what she loves: more people.
The cocktail hour finally arrives: she, like my lovers,
takes my drinks stiff and stuffed in plastic.
My billfold full of rubbers; what else can you do
but lie down with the dogs?

Like my lovers, I used to wake beside
the same body for years: this body
would care for me as a stranger:
fiddle-dee-dee and *poof*: the fantasy
to let this body die young, die with legs in the air:

such a pretty corpse. Soon the scent
of burning leaves is too much.
Edna's slight chest heaves,
her limbs naked, blooming,
barley moon.

Ladies in the street hollering *eggs, eggs, eggs*.

Soutine, your *Carcass*

The butchering
is out of order.
Hung by its hock

on the six hook,
its softness is still
visible. Its skin

yet to be
removed as you
would turn

down a sock;
the entrails
and ribs are doffed,

but from anus
to sternum
its cavity

remains. Your eye
follows this slit
to its head,

and look!
Its own little eyes
stare away

and it reveals
its perfect
little teeth.

Rilke, your garden

Sudden harshness
of a winter snow.
Sundial's shadow-
hand ticks softly
against the porous
gray stone. Empty
trees. All is fallen.
It wanted to
remain intact:
leaves to branches,
umbels of wild
carrot, fennel.
*How one feels
a small life's shortness,*
yet one still feels
the vastness past
the ha-ha's mark.
*You don't survive in me
because of memories;*
and he returned
to breaking frozen
soil. Everything is long
gone. The west, now
yellow and violet,
reminded him
of something
once living, warm:
the last green
touching blue.

—That one winter when it snowed everywhere.

The island we once inhabited is now winter clay;
not-so-quite-nights—the hours set back to no-about-to-turn,
of mistaking a man who owns the same blue hat for you.
Are you still wearing that green coat?

Someone's legs spread beneath you, her Rogue shirt, her face
profiled as if to say *look*. And the snow freshly falling here
as it is there, as it is where you are, always getting higher.
What time does your transit ticket say?

You have an other: a small, red-haired girl
standing on a fallen evergreen, hair like fire
when it catches light—she is balanced, ethereal.
You do love the cliché, the familiar shackle
to keep your heart together.

You eat her salads with daikon, zucchini blossoms,
symmetrically cut butternut squash, and say words
that begin with the first two letters of your name:
p*hunny*, *phantastic*, *phaithful*, and she *phell* into it,
bit into as if it were a mountain apple.

—

There is a town 131 miles across the Lahaina Roads
with black sands that was once abandoned for 50 years,
unreachable, uninhabitable.

Further back, the lehua blossoms we planted.
Their sepals are now bare.
Perhaps this is metaphorical.

Men in canvas jackets sweep the snow from the sidewalk
and a girl rides her bicycle between the maples.

Sometimes the light filters through the clouds.
Sometimes the light that filters through the clouds is warm.

We are frost situated on the stoop of a convenience store
that looks like that one we'd go to
purchase the small things you had forgotten.

Pastime: A narrative

Let me tell you a story of a girl
who worked in a field, growing organic tomatoes,
who later tried to tip a cow on her way home
in a neighboring field one afternoon: it mooed
and kept walking away and she followed it
still pressing her hand on its side.
The girl kept pressing harder and harder
until she lost her balance and fell in a puddle.

That night she cried. She began downloading videos
of boys trying to tip cows in the fields

where, late at night, they drank their parents' beer.
Eventually they started to throw the empty bottles
at the cows' heads and the boys would laugh
as the cows mooed and they all walked away as if nothing happened.
These boys were baseball players in Windsor, Illinois
so they could throw hard, straight, and fast even when drunk.

She moved to Illinois where she tried to find the boys.
Let me call her Edna. Edna wasn't that great.

Sometimes I can almost understand how she must've felt,
that need to push, that need for aggression, that hard desire
for people like her. Understanding has its advantages.
You're in Seattle now, sitting in a hotel, watching TV,
drinking coffee, getting sober, and I'm wondering
if it's only rain blowing off the tops of buildings or if it's really raining.
The understanding of me and you, nearly giving way to the ground,

nearly feeling the give of losing balance by the hour.
It's April now and it's just too late for that feeling to stop.

Edna's Incantation: Or, how I imagine

Edna returned to Mesilla. It was March.
Exactly the 27. She walked the roads
covered in three years worth of sand,
the scent of creosotes caught in the wind.

She searched for the little house I lived in,
but it had disappeared with the rest
of the neighborhood. I wanted that
even if I were still in the house.

She asked about me everywhere,
but oleasters and aphids covered
my tracks too well. She sat down,
hands touching what must have been

the stones of my steps, and screamed
what she had wanted to say—*You
can come with me, there is room now.*

And ants billowed from the ground,
mosquitoes fell from stagnant clouds.
She cried *come with me* directly to the stones,

and felt the sand extend from her,
making what seemed like water.

—There and here

One view from the window, at nightfall,
saying "Abend," as if a prayer to the sky
of mini-lighthouses. Freighter-clouds
in Port Townsend send their regards
to Hilo. The single invitation: Seattle.

Staring at the Westin's curved windows,
I knew you wouldn't be walking down
this street at the end of it all. But here
in West Fork I dream of titans & giants,
of a man who weeps at the edge of my bed.

—

I don't dream, I just stay up & want
to leave. Like you, I see gardens of gods,
gods at dusk. Lunar angels that keep the fires
burning, making the land barren.
When I crawl to the edge of my bed, I unlock
your ghost & watch him turn over. I let him turn.

Who are you now? Are you still panicked?
Are you still vulnerable despite your appendages:
head, legs, watch, money? Are you worn-out
I am on my knees, here, speak. "Abend."

—

I'm in a bar at seven in the morning.
I didn't know they opened this early.
Then I try to stop thinking & order
another. The bartender suggests another.
He is in a nightshirt & wonders if he is sad.
Obviously his lover is still sleeping.

Then a sour white liquid comes through the roof.
I am thinking of a rotting Western Larch,
silver geraniums, & how your island grows
42 acres each year. The bartender is still talking
about sadness, but then we high five until I hear
the metallic sound of the universe.

[The day begins in rain]

The day begins in rain. The trains
have stopped running their courses
and the businesses' OPEN signs
no longer glow. The workers
decided to sit in storage sheds
for cigarettes and cups of coffee.
They are cold, tired.

The ground is covered in leaves,
bug carcasses, discarded deli bowls.
A worker discovers how to spell
"cigarette" without autocorrect,
then quietly heads back inside
before the sun burns holes
in the remainder of the night sky.

The day begins in smoke. A red glow
from an OPEN sign now glares
against thick dust of windows
and fingerprints slowly come
into focus on the glass door.
If looked through closely
another world comes into view

for a moment. Fresh brewed coffee
with milk, yesterday's newspaper,
cured meats and varied cheeses.
A worker with trembling hands
empties water from the deli case.
Another rotates the chocolates
and pastries with almonds and figs.

The day begins in wind. Street lamps'
hums grow silent as the moths return
to dark corridors. Their wings drum
against lower sashes of windows. Trains
begin to pull away nocturnal smells
with their departures. Brown fog
billows toward slanted roofs,

stirring leaves from gutters.
Saturated faces exchange fragments
from yesterday. The day begins
and soon it will no longer be October.
The day begins, but it is still difficult
to find total lightness in it. The day's
newspaper spread out on the table.

Trakl Speaks:

The house is empty so autumn has come
to fill the rooms with starless sonata.
There is, it seems, an awakening at the end

of the twilit forest. *You always think
of the white faces of mankind darkening
when the house is empty.* Autumn has come

in, far from the turmoil of a stranger—
my private self—who rises to empty windows;
there is, it seems, an awakening at the end

of evening's silver voice. A green branch bows
willingly. In the distance someone wakes.
This house is empty and autumn has come

like wind's purple arms moving through
the hallway. *I am alone with my murderer.*
Awakening. Moonlight darkening eyelids.

Let go. Cross. Evening speaks now in the garden.
Cover your blue lips. *The young dead walk in
intimate conversation among the elms, down

the green river.* What do you hear from the leaves?
Snuff the candle. The house is empty and awake
with the decay of flesh: the golden shape
of a friend who remained behind.

—I have fantasies about the post office worker on 8th St.

If I have any romantic notions left, please let me mail them
with stamps I will need to purchase. Don't offer me seasonal,
just Forever. Don't comment on my shabby tape job. I don't care
if the box stays together. I would prefer these romantic notions
to scatter from your mail cart, or the mail dock room, or fly
through the mail truck's window in a quick breeze and let them
trash someone's lawn. Don't be kind and feel the need to
tape my box. Don't tell me you've seen worse jobs and this is
what you do for them. These romantic notions don't deserve it.

Let there be another conversation between us instead:
one about the accident that made you limp,
or how many blue shirts you own,
or how many six-packs and cheese sandwiches you ate
when the child support became too much,
or how you had to move in with your cousin and sell the dog.

Let us talk about driving to Paris, AR to be the first to summit
Hog Jaw Mountain so we can be the first to send pictures
to peakery.com. and say *Sooie!* Let us find another town
after that one, a town with an unsubstantial Southern name—
Sweet Home, Sugar Grove—where we can get a room
and a bottle of Old Grandad, where we can watch reruns
on a bedspread that is the color of urine, and where we can't
help ourselves articulate our needs but only press each other
into the worn, discolored mattress to distract us.

—**Assignation**

What else could have been done to avoid
the touching of bodies?
Shifts of directions that kept us
employed on others more or less
beneficial?

As time would have it,
my repetition of apologies,
your repetition of to be continueds,
command even a little bit of light.
Love, this light prevents a downfall

but stronger air is needed to feed it.
Already I find a lack of it. And there
you are, hands cupping that little flame
you have to offer in the stillest hours,
till I awoke and remembered the dark
interior that keeps me from dreaming
your face and the quiet falling of rain.

But afterwards:

You should have said that you were in love in those years.
I was long past my 30th year. You were not yet 27.
I could not swear to you, only hold your nakedness and say I can
fit my hands around your softness. You then could not swear to me,
only kiss my neck and say sometimes it is lonely.

The desert air embraced us both then, so we could not
abandon ourselves completely: those who could not
continue loving, if maybe too quietly.

Remember that night when we left the party early
and saw a mutt twacked by a car? Body rolling
from tire to tire, rattling a singular note until
the night returned to what it had been. Still.
As we were still. Except for the slight pivot
of shadow carrying, what seemed an empty harness.

Someone somewhere must be making love, you said.

Sometimes my hands still feel your nakedness.
Sometimes my neck still feels your lips, sometimes
I say it can be lonely when the cold air breaks through creosotes.

But a woman's nakedness is only nakedness, as is a man's,
and I—I say all this knowing that the cold air is just the air
and what goodbye actually means. What letting go actually allows.

—Continuum

Four times you woke, as if in other beds, as if in other places.
The first was mine with damp sheets, off-white, salt-caked,
from when in the Pacific our navels met. And I wanted to keep you
dreaming, wandering among anthurium and protea gone tame.

But you woke, and said for days you heard the myna speak your
          name
from a narrow opening that led to stairs of coral, which led to a small
          beach.
There was a gap in the sand overfilled with rotting fish and
          driftwood,
under a half-risen sun that caused your skin to become a stranger's
          skin.

You drifted back to that waning island of your own life
because, by the fourth time you woke, I knew you
would always wake as if in other beds, as if in other places,
as if a stranger who answers to the same name darkness left behind.

Trakl, your self-portrait

Black fits.
Aesthetic:
the cuck-
oo's lament
constructed
to countenance.
Black-mold
gaze toward
a flame
that's snuffed,
sealing red
like a scar
of a birth-wound.
Lament, figure!
decay looms
as if all roads
lead toward
the harrowing
cry of your
blood-animal.

Before the autopsy

It's the modesty of a naked body
under the sheet. The tongue
touching the back of teeth.

For my brother

I thought that it rained here

I thought that I rose from
the bed
I had been avoiding
for weeks
with the TV off

I went to the window

As a child
in Missouri
I was warned at school
not to cross rising water

As a child
I was told
high water is
not trite
in central Missouri
not trite along its river

They say on the news
Boston is under
three feet of snow
three more is to be expected

A young man is declared
dead in his home eight hours
after being released
from the ER
it will be 46 degrees

And I
will listen to each of my alarms go off

[I will die in a Walmart parking lot]

I will die in a Walmart parking lot wearing sweatpants.
I remember the day I bought those sweatpants. I was in Walmart
pushing a shopping cart I didn't need and saw the sweatpants
clipped to an extra-large hanger. They were a medium but who cares
about sizes for sweatpants?

It was a Wednesday when I bought the sweatpants,
so I will die in a Walmart parking lot on a Wednesday.
I am writing this on a Wednesday in a Walmart café
so it is only fitting that I die in a Walmart parking lot
on a Wednesday wearing sweatpants I bought from Walmart
on a Wednesday.

I will be hit by a car driving too fast for it to be a Wednesday
and not a Sunday. And my sweatpants will slip below my butt cheeks
because I am a size small, not a medium.

This will be caught on security cameras but because it is a
        Wednesday,
not a Tuesday or a Thursday no one will see the footage for 24 hours.
And because the car that hit me was actually backing up, not pulling
        in,
I will go unnoticed to the driver so dying is really something one
        does alone.

Did I mention I will die in a Walmart parking lot at 4 am because I
        was alone
and bored in my apartment? I will die in a Walmart parking lot
        because I was
alone and bored in my apartment and decided to saunter to the
        florescent lights
to buy a bag of potato chips. Edna died in a Walmart parking lot
technically for a bag of potato chips. Probably some dip to go with
        them too.

And my friends will call me *fatass*. But once they see the security
      footage
of my exposed butt cheeks that slipped out from my oversized
      sweatpants,
I may get called *flatass*. But because I was run over in a Walmart
      parking lot,
a flatass is a given

within their constructed pastoral

When the deer venture from the woods,
they carry the morning over Sunset Hill by strings
tied to their telemets,
and because the deer descend
to eat the young grass, the morning, too, rests

by the stately, iron-fenced plots. The settling
of this light breaks the soil into boxelders,

until the sound mimics the moving water
over Cave Hollow's sandstone edges.

In the distance the Aeolian harp's deep octaves hum
through the red oak branches, eddying new
and indifferent leaves,
while the bronze children
at Memorial Park grow colder and less recognizable

beneath the shadows of the city around them.
Within their constructed pastoral, mouths open

in the shape of laughter, they will not ripen
into their oversized teeth.

Notes

<u>The Afters, Imitations and Departures:</u>

"[You think of an Island]," "[When you arrived]," and "But afterwards:" are after Donald Justice. See his poems "Speaking of Islands" and "On the Night of the Departure by Bus," specifically in his *Collected Poems* (04). "On the Night of the Departure by Bus" is noted as "loosely based in structure on poems by Rafael Alberti."

"[And we've slept for too long]," "—Continuum," and "Edna's Incantation: Or, how I imagine" are a departure and loose imitations of Tomasz Różycki's "And so the War," "Other Places," and "Scorched Maps," translated by Mira Rosenthal, which can be found in the 2007 collection *Forgotten Keys*. Certain lines from the sources have been repurposed to create a new narrative.

"There and here" was inspired by Tomaž Šalamun's "Dolmen," translated by Christopher Merrill.

"Pastime: A narrative" is an imitation of "Found and Lost" by Robert Long.

"For my brother" is dedicated to James Boston, who died in 2015. The poem itself stems from frequent readings of Franz Wright's *Ill Lit* (98), and uses a variant on the line "High water is not trite in southern Ohio. Nothing is trite along a river" from James Wright's "Honey."

"[I will die in a Walmart parking lot]" is based off Cesar Vallejo's "Black Stone Lying on a White Stone," translated by Robert Bly.

<u>The Ekphrastics and the Centos:</u>

"Edna: Sleeping at Grand Isle" is based on the painting *Sleeping Woman*, 1849 by Johann Baptist Reiter.

"Small Cento: Edna finds a lover for tonight" is made of lines from D.A. Powell's poems "the cocktail hour finally arrives: whether ending a day at the office," "this is what you love: more people. you remember," "he would care for me as a stranger: courtesy clerk. so quick," "writing for a young man on the redline train: 'to his boy mistress,'" "winter moon summer moon budding moon barley moon," "a happiest harbinger to you: here spring," "chapt. ex ex ex eye vee: in which scott has a birthday," "dogs and boys can treat you like trash. and dogs do love trash," "12-line poem, seemingly out of place," and "19 lines," which appear in his 2004 collection *Cocktails*. Pronouns have been altered and lines have been repurposed to create a new narrative thread.

"12-line poem, seemingly out of place" in the source material is noted to end with a line from a John Waters movie, and thus makes an appearance in "Small Cento: Edna finds a lover for tonight" as well.

"Soutine, your *Carcass*" is based on the painting *Carcass of Beef*, 1924 by Chaim Soutine.

"Rilke, your garden" is based on "Interior Portrait," his letters, and "Blue Hydrangea."

"Trakl Speaks:" uses lines from "To the One Short-Lived," translated by James Reidel, "Horror" and "Hohenburg," translated by Daniel Simko.

"Trakl, your self-portrait" is based on *Self Portrait*, 1913 by Georg Trakl.

Thank Yous

Thank you to the English Department and Creative Writing Program at the University of Central Missouri, especially to Wayne Miller, Charles Martin, Celia Kingsbury, Kevin Prufer, Marc McKee, Kathryn Nuernberger, and Don Melichar. Your continued and wonderful support is invaluable to me. Thank you to Centrum and the Port Townsend Writers Conference (and all its ghosts) for providing me the space to explore, engage, discuss, and disappear. I would like to extend a special thank you to its once but always fearless leader Jordan Hartt. Without his hard work in maintaining the community, I would still be searching. Thank you to Dana Levin, Gary Copeland Lilley, and Carl Phillips for their generous workshops and discussions, to Katrina Stubson and Susan Landgraf, and to everyone I have met and exchanged conversations with while there. Thank you, too, to friends, colleagues, and support in Las Cruces, NM and the University of Arkansas in Fayetteville, especially to Bob Sholl, Ed O'Casey, Molly Bess Rector, and Elian Mota. And an extended thank you to Rodney Jones and Geffrey Davis. Our time was brief but helpful and insightful. Thank you also to Sara Burge, Michael Czyzniejewski, Nina Dellaria, and Sahar Mustafah.

I end with love and the biggest thanks to my family and Patrick Tucker.

Melissa Boston is originally from Sedalia, MO and currently lives in Fayetteville, AR with the artist Patrick Tucker. She attended the University of Central Missouri and, after a brief intermission in New Mexico, the University of Arkansas. Her poetry has appeared in several literary journals, including *Moon City Review, Midwestern Gothic,* and *Raleigh Review*.

www.ingramcontent.com/pod-product-compliance
Lightning Source LLC
LaVergne TN
LVHW041600070426
835507LV00011B/1213